THE WHITE FIRE OF TIME

Also by Ellen Hinsey

Cities of Memory

ELLEN HINSEY

THE WHITE FIRE
OF TIME

Wesleyan University Press

MIDDLETOWN CONNECTICUT

Published 2002
Wesleyan University Press
110 Mt. Vernon Street
Middletown, CT 06459
Printed in the United States of America

∞ The paper used in this publication meets the requirements of the
American National Standard for Information Sciences — Permanence
of Paper for Printed Library Materials, ANSI z39.48–1984

Library of Congress Cataloging-in-Publication Data

Hinsey, Ellen, 1960–
    The white fire of time / Ellen Hinsey.
        p. cm. — (Wesleyan poetry)
    ISBN 0-8195-6556-3 (cloth : alk. paper) — ISBN 0-8195-6557-1
(pbk. : alk. paper)
    I. Title. II. Series.
    PS3558.I5469 W47 2002
    811'.54 – dc21   2002006174

This world is one and the same world

ODYSSEUS ELYTIS

Contents

Acknowledgments

Grateful acknowledgment is made to the following periodicals, in which selections of this work previously appeared: *Poetry:* "On the Hours in the Night Garden," "On a Short History of Chance," and "From the Book on the Nature of Things"; *The Southern Review:* "On a Panel of Adam Naming the Animals," "On a Miniature from the Sacred Ark," "On the Night of the Second Day," and "On the Endurance of the Flesh of the World"; *Poetry Review* (London): "On Varieties of Flight" and "On the Life of Decay"; *The New England Review:* "On the Uncountable Nature of Things"; *The Missouri Review:* "Thirteen Aphorisms on the Nature of Evil," "On the Struggle with the Angel," "On the Dream of the Celestial Ladder," "On Feeling that the Dead are Near," and "On the 13 Rungs of Sorrow"; *Jubilat:* "On Abraham Receiving the Sacred Language"; *Leviathan Quarterly:* "On the Unique Cosmology of Passion." Some of these poems also appeared in translation: *Berlin Tagesspiegel:* "Thirteen Aphorisms on the Nature of Evil" in translation "Dreizehn Aphorismen über die Natur des Bösen"; *Revue de Belles Lettres:* "On the Struggle with the Angel" in translation "Sur la lutte avec l'ange," and "Thirteen Aphorisms on the Nature of Evil" in translation "Treize aphorismes sur la nature du mal."

"On the Struggle with the Angel," "On the Creation of the Golem," "Thirteen Aphorisms on the Nature of Evil," and "On the Unlanguageable Name of God" also appeared in Paris in a limited fine arts edition entitled *The Temple* with etchings by Khoa Pham.

For their generous support during the time this book was written,
the author would like to thank The Chateau de Lavigny,
The Rona Jaffe Foundation Writers' Awards
and The Lannan Foundation.

PART ONE

THE WORLD

I.

Meditation

ON THE UNCOUNTABLE NATURE OF THINGS

I.

Thus, not the thing held in memory, but this:
      The fruit tree with its scars, thin torqued branches;

The high burnished sheen of morning light
      Across its trunk; the knuckle-web of ancient knots,

II.

The swift, laboring insistence of insects—
      Within, the pulse of slow growth in sap-dark cores,

And the future waiting latent in fragile cells:
      The last, terse verses of curled leaves hanging in air—

And the dry, tender arc of the fruitless branch.

III.

Yes: the tree's spine conditioned by uncountable
      Days of rain and drought: all fleeting coordinates set

Against a variable sky—recounting faithfully
   The thing as it is—transient, provisional, changing

Constantly in latitude—a refugee not unlike
   Us in this realm of exacting, but unpredictable, time.

IV.

And only once a branch laden with perfect
   Fruit—only once daybreak weighed out perfectly by

The new bronze of figs, *not things in memory,*
   But as they are here: the roar and plough of daylight,

The perfect, wild cacophony of the present—
   Each breath measured and distinct in a universe ruled

V.

By particulars—each moment a universe:
   As when under night heat, passion sparks—unique,

New in time, and hands, obedient, divine,
   As Desire dilates eye—pulse the blue-veined breast,

Touch driving, forging the hungering flesh:
   To the far edge of each moment's uncharted edge—

VI.

For the flesh too is earth, desire storm to the marrow—
        Still—*the dream of simplicity in the midst of motion*:

Recollection demanding a final tallying of accounts,
        The mind, loyal clerk, driven each moment to decide—

Even as the tree's wood is split and sweat still graces
        The crevices of the body, which moment to weigh in,

For memory's sake, on the mobile scales of becoming.

II.

Reading

ON VARIETIES OF FLIGHT

There, in the air—traceless blue—arena of circuits
    And saunters, some rise with difficulty

        While others lift buoyant, tack of tail turned
            Westward—take wide air under their keel,

And sprint, shoot and sail up to where, in invisible
    Gyres they revolve tropical or northern,

        Spreading their full breadth to survey the scene,
            Their prey hidden in land folded and patched;

Others, tail-sure tuck and dive, fall in a single tear,
    Against a stony silhouette of hill; others

        In wind jibe and yaw, storm-wise, head into
            Air as prows take the jab and flack of waves—

But some are threaded by thin parachute, line of silk,
    They soar only when bidden, cross a width

        Of draft, but hang when the wind is becalmed
            And suspended; still others come from deeper

Hues—leap into air as if seeking a higher realm,
   Where hidden stars crown a miraculous

      Dome of blue—fly on their fins, and their short
         Leap is the curve of Noah's colored arc:

Still for others, flight is trammeled—rooted, as fires lift
   Only in sparks, but are held fast to their

      Flames; and sound flies blindly over distance,
         But cannot renew the force of its thrust;

Sight sweeps and tempers rise; tall grasses bend and
   Rumors mount; winds wind over, as insects

      Hover, and stars speed free under frail falling
         Night, while fleet tongues tell their tales—

      And Knowledge—poor earth-bound ember—sails,
         But fails to ignite.

(a)

"Here in the body this subtle, impalpable, invisible one known as 'Person', begins to move, or rather a fraction . . . does, though there was no awareness beforehand, just as when a sleeper awakes . . ."

III.

Fragment

ON THE ORIGINS OF CONSCIOUSNESS

Buried in the depths of that great forest called *childhood*, under a constellation of leaves whose stars cast shadows down from their heaven—there, on a day in late summer, emerging from that wood, one came upon—startled—the fragile *I*, loitering unawares: stumbled upon like a benevolent stranger who stared back dumbfounded—

In that green, limpid silence, the self *the self* regarded—in that moment of new knowledge, and suddenly aware, the *I* itself scrutinized: stomach, knees, teeth, knuckles, hair—a devout inventory was made. There among the burgeoning branches, all distinct features and flaws were duly laid out that day, for careful inspection, and all impressions imprinted on the waiting clay of the mind.

All elements for an early hypothesis of being.

But then—the self thought—the *I* must be tested. So there by the roadside, under the transparent light of shame, while ants slowly inspected the foot's arch, the self *on itself* conducted a further interrogation filled with arguments of delicate logic and counter-logic and hypotheses of sure disappointment—

It was thus that conclusions were drawn: though the *I* was persuasive, capable of insight and precise sensation, contained in flesh as it was, it was unable to retain even one full instant of being. In every moment—regardless of season—it pruned back the thicket of wonder. Each night, unfailingly, chastened by memory in the small room of sleep: recollection returning to the *I* with its arms full of all the precious, abandoned images.

Still, the *I* protested: it yearned to make use of its modest store of being—fulfilled only, it came to dream, under the protection of love's arbor. *Simply that*, the *I* argued—casting before it its long, thin shadow: the desire to lie down with *You* under its wild, forked lightning.

IV.

Meditation

I.

Before dawn, in the still-dark, under the great obscurity,
                    Which is ruled by planets—the mighty nebulas,

The twisting spheres of beaten rock, with their particles
                    Of dust and fiery gases; there in the blackness,

Your bodies turn together—witnesses to night's tender
                    Gravity: you gather momentum from the ancient

Constellations, draw your synchrony from air, embrace
                    In that dark where the body's arch becomes the

Night's twin hemisphere, and love establishes its order—

The body, impatient, tires of its limits, demands to be led
                    Into that universe of heat: where sweat and spine

Bind in a unity of knowledge that the flesh alone knows—
                    For the body—singular, perishable—harbors

13

Its intimate fears: to remain still amidst motion, to never
    Be touched—to never near the one center where

Time, excluded, must watch—skin wishes to be driven
    Alive, the pulse to hammer its stay, the cell's fire

Be engulfed in that dark where the mysteries once lay—

II.

For greater than shame—is to not be called into being,
    By the desire of another's hand, not to near that

Wild chaos where life's power endures—commands:
    Tonight, entwined, your need bruising the flesh,

You advance toward that which holds all matter in
    Its grip: ride into that essence which is energy's

Core—reach toward where all beginnings roil again
    Their ore, and as in the Earth—so in the body all

Precious release waits: now finally, willingly, submit
    To all contained in breath—

Labor resolutely past day's heft and rubble: near that
    Great love in which one might fuse and bind—

And cry out under a mantle of sweat—in a temper
    Of want, temper of desire—in that hour when need

And loss lie together: undo the stubborn boundaries
                Of flesh. Let the heart in its tight captivity beat then

Its joyful rage—while your limbs which are joined
                Together in love—lift, climb, try mindlessly to rise—

But face their limits in that—*yes, surely*, faultless air.

V.

Commentary

ON THE WEIGHT OF DAILINESS

α.

On an afternoon when—*today*—noon is unannounced,
        Yet divides the spheres of day into memory and waiting;

β.

In these hollow moments, when all flesh is found arbitrary,
        And arbitrary all the details of regret or expectation—

γ.

One might imagine rain, but instead time rushes the window;
        Again, wind at the window?—no, just a river of minutes.

δ.

In the green stasis of silence: an eclipse of intent.
        The self, unmoored, slowly rides the camber of daylight.

ε.

Start again, try—rouse the idle machine of the body.
        In the silence—perhaps: strange intimations of foreboding.

ζ.

What then, can reaffirm the just sovereignty of being?

The mind's logic: a bridge in the air that no step follows.

η.

You are suddenly patient with folly; tire of nostalgia.

The first human, the second: seeds sown in the wind's salt.

θ.

You dream of distraction, to drag you towards evening.

Outside, a squall, without intent or rancor, flails the trees.

ι.

Finally you would speak: pry open the vault of silence.

Your voice's clamor: the harsh laboring of a wooden bell.

ϰ.

In late afternoon, memory rises like carp from a muddied pool.

Memory escapes capture: the shadowy forms stay buried.

λ.

Daylight, once again vanquished, burns red on the far horizon.

The body—pierced by loneliness—would shed its flesh.

μ.

And the heart, distant—painfully remote—seemingly unused.

But in loyalty, practicing all afternoon its common work.

(b)

"... *Every process is partially or totally interfered with by chance, so much so that ... a course of events absolutely conforming to specific laws is almost an exception ...*"

VI.

Fragment

ON A SHORT HISTORY OF CHANCE

It is said that Aristotle did not believe that nature needed chance to begin. And Augustine, freed from such deliberations, was sure God was at the heart of the patent, as well as the obscure, occurrence. To look once into the Divine Face was to have the great map of destiny spread out: complete with the body's tidal currents, the slow lamentation of flowers, the cyclical reign of the seasons, and the soul's knowledge.

But in time, the sure, steady mind clarified: it was the mechanical wheel of the universe that would prevail—its gyroscope of history advancing perfectly as it swallowed time. Thus, freed from sacrifice, the works of labor, not conscience, would fulfil the great collective destiny; all species carefully noted in the mighty encyclopedias of being, entered by a steady but passionless hand.

Yet listening at each daybreak—the unknown still came dropping outside of the bright, clear realms. Invariably returning, as it manifested in sudden apparition or by silent stealth: as still in wonder the senses are caught up when the sea delivers—but once—a wave of pure ivory—or etched in salt is a cathedral of the world.

Or how a face, long lost, appears on a street swimming up out of a crowd, as if from a foreign element. What, if not chance, holds all of these fast in its grip? The moment—great abyss of now: bearing the fruit of all moments before, ripe with disorganized creation.

VII.

Reading

ON THE LIFE OF DECAY

Enmeshed in each moment—the green river of lichen
    Advances, undoes, the kingdom of surety;

    There—in a basin of darkness—below the edge
        Of light-level, where shadows cover wood's

Endurance—in that sea of air—in a jade air of undoing,
    Moisture robes each leaf left in the entombed

    Damp of a valley, under the crossed helix of
        Branches, crevasses alive with still water:

The trail of moss along the forest floor's dimensions,
    The mosaic of virus—inhabiting the cells—

    The incessant love of parasites, turning in their
        Toil, under the tight screen of ivy's stars—

Or above, the parched length of an old branch, dangling;
    The air biting, devouring, in its feast of removal—

    Up on the hillside, the gale's caress chastening
        The rock face, seeking out with its brutal hand

The boiled surface of rust on the junked empty wagon,
Bending a hinge as it swings into an empty berth:

Whittling the roof's thatch, lifting the smoke of dry rot
In waves, hammering the headland's old profile—

Until it lifts to observe lands gullied and bared; surveys fans
Of sand run by rain, beat by sun—watches as

Sodden soil, weight of earth once held in mass,
Brings down hills suddenly to the mouth of the sea—

Here in each moment—water's endless song of erosion,
And the terrible attack of the wind's undertow:

Yes, the fast building crescendo, the vast knowledge
Amassing, the return and holy rebuilding—

Of the great, the final, temple of air.

INTERMEZZO

FROM THE BOOK ON THE NATURE OF THINGS

Intermezzo

In the Beginning

Chaos: mass without master, substance uncontrolled by subject. The unintelligible force of the world.

The Human Abyss

The human soul where all opposites contend; thus chaos always newly and furtively forming.

What then is the Body?

A passing handprint; a thin wave in the voice of time.

Bargaining with Time

Futility of discourse. A rage of wind in the trees.

Grave Discomfort

The prison of self-consciousness. Insomnia of the ego.

The Sensation of Grace

To be like a fish suspended in a net, caught up in the web of the world.

Temptation Disguised as Thought
To follow an argument, abstractly, to its conclusion.

Intuitive Conjecture
The suspicion of the inconsequence of being.

Perplexing Fact
Imagination, itinerant, travels independent of us, performing in all of the provinces.

Premature Sorrow
The violation of trust by knowledge.

Startling Insights
Words that seek an entry into the flesh, as if to return to their origins.

What is Remembered
The loam of dusk rising under the luminous bow of summer.

Maturity of Sorts

To abandon simplicity and climb the tilted ladder of paradox.

The Sensation of Nostalgia

Unexplained night winds; a chill patterned with longing.

Where does the Soul Reside?

Under the cover of darkness, having been routed by evil.

The Pursuit of the Good

To find out where the soul is hiding from evil.

Forgetfulness of Objects

The mirror's silver which forgets, even quicker than the mind, the green ripeness of apples.

Concluding Hypothesis

And then, if the soul exists—what a thicket it lives in!

PART TWO

THE TEMPLE

VIII.

Meditation

ON A PANEL OF ADAM NAMING THE ANIMALS

I.

One must remember: all around was Wonder.
                    And each entity caught that glint and glowed

Under the particularity of its nature. Him—
                    Seated beneath the noble oak in glorious leaf

Full aloft—pronouncing each syllable in deft
                    Voice and sure of its apt transubstantiation:

II.

Doe—legs of quick draw and drum-colored
                    Breast—all *Cervidae*, blessed with springing

And spirit colonized by humble ruminating—
                    Then—the birds resting on that singular hand:

Spreading wing or turning breast to suggest
                    Hidden crimson play in that most precious

III.

Etymology. Trancelike fish floated in the ether
                Of air, while below, battalions of ants awaited

Their collective calling. Beast, fish, fowl, they
                Filed past, on webbed foot or woolly haunch,

Each name pulled from the surest source like
                The plume-tail of smoke from a volcanic heart.

IV.

By evening Adam lay finally tired: each utterance
                Had been of such consequence. He lay still

At the base of the glorious oak, precious clover
                Sewn tightly beneath his head. And closed

His eyes to all pleasures, so great had been his
                Labors. For he was human—in the Garden.

V.

Yet despite his careful setting of each appellative
                Stone in that arch, which was atopped by God,

Midnight found him struck—*dolor mortalis*—
                In his mind he saw how the spirit thumps and

Tears at the fabric of a word's small tent—
                And learned his lesson that *to name* is man's

VI.

Unique tautology. He turned his face then
                    In the coal-bright dark—in molten shame—

From that of God's: for he knew his swift
                    Tongue flawed and approximative—it alone

Lacked the precise, assured syntax of flight.

IX.

Reading

ON A MINIATURE FROM THE SACRED ARK
(Adam in the Garden)

Rough tree, my Adam, your knotted, slender body
    Is my Garden—*you*, whose first, curved flank

        Energy brought to Being—you, with your lean
            Trunk of middle and firm-mapped Backside,

The planetary continent of your warmth—Wild-horse
    Buttocks, feet great-weight bearing, topped by

        Your agile neck of Birch, *unique:* the fine-etched
            Ivory work of your eyes, jewel-set by

Your pupil's dark eclipse—at rest, your loins: a grove
    Of sweet cedar, and sweat falling to your sex

        Clings as tendrils twine the late grape clusters—
            For pleasure has been ours in the Garden.

When you return from the field's path with clay-dust
    On your lids—your skin ruddy from the sun's

        Heat—Let us lie, making the rush-clad hill
            Our bedstraw, and find not red thorn that

Grows in waste: the lacework of your tributary veins,
  The tight-latticed, green timber of your ribs;

  Take me in your arms, the sound weight of earth—
    For here in innocence, we are released from time.

Though, my Beloved, time will close on us like slow,
  Wind-cooled wax. But, let us not speak of that—

  For where flesh is joined together the harvest
    Endures—hold me under the great granite

Sky, in this pass of night: where birds, restless stars, hang
  In the far, high trees, and even the ragged mouse

  Has not crumbs of shame to satisfy his hunger.
    For, like you, I too wish for eternity—

  Come to me again that we might hide another
    Night from knowledge.

(c)

"An angel of God taught him Hebrew, the language of revelation, by which he was enabled to decipher all the secrets of the ancient books . . ."

X.

Fragment

ON ABRAHAM RECEIVING THE SACRED LANGUAGE

It was early morning, and daylight had not yet settled on the furrows of the field like a silent bird. He felt something lift the blanket of sleep—and whether from within or without—he followed those swift currents of air to the edge of the field and sat, his feet in the dirt, awaiting first light.

There, in meditation, his hand was drawn forth by a grace-filled gravity, and across the etched surface of the earth—which was now lit golden by dawn-rays—he drew his stick twice across. He made the shape of one bird's wing, held upright as if against a racing wind. And as through this he drew a second line, a sound came to his lips: he spoke a whisper in the air that was the sure utterance of the tongue's prayer.

His mouth shaped and unshaped a succession of sounds, and he guarded each one in his spirit like jewels sewn closely into a precious cloth—*alef, bet, g'imel* . . . they shone in his mind, and he divined that in them he would find first wisdom. In his amazement, he had not realized that morning was complete—and afternoon now cast her lengthening shadows against his feet. But then, his stirring had been stilled—and his soul lay silent in its own heat, the way a field in full grain burns abruptly under the sun, when abandoned by wind.

He shook the dirt from his legs, and started back to the tents, when, in the mirage of the distance he thought he saw cities in flames, and the voices of the innocent, crying out from their chains—or rising in a column of cindered air. *Makat shemesh—heat dreams*, he thought, as he reached his tent, and bending down in the present, he did not see

The blue shadow of his tribe's future trail after him.

XI.

Commentary

ON THE STORY OF CAIN AND ABEL

The first difference of kind from those same cells:
                    Firstborn followed by similitude—

But inexact: multiplication bringing marvel,
          But also bearing divergence: hence variance, rival,
                                        broil,

Cain said to Abel his brother, "Let us go out to the field."

The wide inch of dissimilitude of skin: the difference of most
          Intimate parameters—
                              chasm of particulars,

And how experience sews foreignness to flesh—
          And sin by envy, even for those limbs wrought

And when they were in the field, Cain rose up against his brother

                              From the same crucible of spirit.
But what difference?
          Eyes and hands, sweat-soiled muscle and
                              tongue's bitter thirst—

And killed him.

But thought, not body, is sin—opposes similitude:

The mind, directed by the cell's division,
                              Turns to detail in its frailty,
And the fragile atom of impulse—

Then the Lord said to Cain, "Where is Abel your brother?"

The mind, spite-harborer, is so inclined—compelled to let
                Instinct sway,
                              Consents to fulfill its unmindful intent—

The voice of your brother's blood is crying to me from the ground—

Temptation—to indulge in difference:
                For in wild dreams of difference first home is lost—

And nowhere will you find your kin—for as necessity split the
        cells in two,
It is for mind to mend itself
                        Rent by imagined dissimilitude—

Until then, you shall be a fugitive, and a wanderer on the earth.

XII.

Meditation

ON THE STRUGGLE WITH THE ANGEL

I.

Suddenly, in the heat-weight of summer afternoon,
        When stalks of bleached grain near their sacrifice,

Knowledge tells you—*yes*—this shape that comes,
        Under the cover of beech shadow, by the stream,

You have met before; you swear you know this sharp
        Harvest breath—as once bending in shade you

Felt a presence near—or when from road-black light
        Shimmered once—and made one ask if all that

Rises invisible—disappears—

Or perhaps was it from the depth of a half-hewn sleep,
        When trailed by dreams you heard a fettered voice,

And waking quickly made your accounts—with *did*—
        Or *had*—in that ledger which hangs by night above

Your head, and details all your choices—*No*—you know
                This frame, which at close view could be yours—

The same—and resolute you square there, by the water
                As you had failed to do in those thatch-dark hours,

Though now, as then, you know yourself unequal to its
                Power—

II.

For with a resolute strength it has found you out,
                Long-tired, it has watched you count out your sheaf

Of days, unable in the end to separate the chaff
                From the holy—but tonight, under the leafèd sky,

One more time you will try, and weigh this
                Weightless bulk against your back—locked together

You will stand, then—hammer, roll—lunge and
                Sway, until routed by its sure advance, reptant you

Will stagger back—but still hold fast to this frame
                Which could be no other—

And no more separate than the body to its breath.
                This angel—*now*—come to test your strength, knows

You part of the nature of beings who rarely rise
                    To transcend the earth—and as such will fall too—

With the harvest of things.
                    Still tonight—wrestle—face to face, pierce the gaze

That by you alone is driven—for alone you will
                    Face its roar and fire, as you struggle to make good

With all that is given.

XIII.

Commentary

THIRTEEN APHORISMS ON THE NATURE OF EVIL

I.

The unconscious hand of Evil loves its own innocence.

2.

Evil lives for the existence of "the other"; for itself it prefers a familiar, common existence.

3.

Evil always owns its own orchard, and sits there gaily picking cherries.

4.

Evil loves the shape of the human hand, formed like its own; for that sublimely simple tool is capable of carrying out the most monstrously delicate atrocities.

5.

In antiquity, Time begot Chaos. But from Chaos, surely, there arose Evil: for in Chaos there is ambiguity—and Darkness and Night—the home of human regret.

6.

Temptation is made flesh by the love it borrows from the heart.

7.

The will must challenge temptation as memory challenges oblivion.

8.

The brave make a place at their table for Evil. For only first-hand knowledge of evil can transform meditation into action.

9.

Evil is always waiting for opportunity's welcome: thriving as it does on the dark of judgment's eclipse.

10.

Time must tolerate the shape of Evil as it tolerates all other miracles.

11.

Evil loves its house, which it shares with history, which is blind.

12.

One must never forget that history does not exist.
Rather, only consciousness, which makes an imaginary house for time past.

13.

And consciousness is the only sword which makes Evil tremble.

(d)

"He then takes virgin soil from a mountain which has not been dug by men, soaks it in water from a well and makes the Golem, forming each limb by reciting alphabetical permutations . . ."

XIV.

Fragment

ON THE CREATION OF THE GOLEM

Elijah Baal Shem of Chelm has told us how with
virgin earth man brought to being—another being, like
himself, but stuffed with sinews as one might fill a stall
with straw—this half-being, mass of flesh, thus needed
life, if it was to serve its master. And so upon its brow, or
under its lip, the sacred words of the Lord were fixed.

This done, man had indeed made another being to do
his bidding—or so he thought—as servant or slave, and
thus patched together by blood and word, the Golem,
newly freed in human form, set forth. But fired by life, the
Golem, reckless, strode and sought to replace his master.
Indeed, rather than in glorious praise, the Golem prowled
in anxious rage, seeking only to consolidate his power.

He soon built roads that cut through villages and
released cart loads of timber in the air. Under his eye wars
were celebrated in full regalia, while loved ones were shot,
without ceremony, at close range.

Thus the Golem fouled his nest, and soon bands of
Golems roamed the cities making business deals; they
learned how to sell their brother's souls and laced the cities
with metal structures; and having lost track of who was
real—and fearing the identity of the other—they locked
themselves firmly in their cells until they could discern the
first light of morning.

But, in these matters, can the Golem be blamed? For, one must admit, he was only imitating his master. Yes, hadn't it been his master who—not content with what had been freely given—had sought to improve upon his own image, until in the mirror bending low, neither could he see the Sacred Name, which, after all,

Had first been written on his brow.

XV.

Reading

You, my beloved, are all of the earth's wonders:
Your pulse the flicker of watered sunlight

And your cells are the sacred architecture of bees;
Your palm the frail, veiled
mirror of mica

And your skin blemished as the markings of a lily;
Your spine the slow rise of the
amaryllis

For day is still luminous.

And your joints the perfect knots of the cypress;
Your ears the winding path to the mysteries

And your veins the praise of color through marble;
Your knees the sweetness of
first-fallen fruit

And your breasts fragrant as opened summer grain;
Your thumb's print the cosmos and
the world—

My only one, your skin's darkness is my day's rest
As branch shadow
protects the field's edge

Your warmth is the thin veil to cover our sleep
As tendrils are protected
by a blossom's sheath

Your breath the succulent chaos of ripe spring air
As the orchard
lifts the wine-scent
of pears

For time is still luminous.

Your hands, in dreams, the melancholy flight of birds
As dusk-sadness
longs for summer's return

Your cry the call which parts the horizon's wide air
As blue space is
divided by a single white sail

Your thighs the center where time is again renewed
As fallow becomes
full at desire's single
word

And, my beloved, among the brambles and the night—

Your voice is the water of consolation.

XVI.

Meditation

ON THE UNLANGUAGEABLE NAME OF GOD

Under the thunderous silence, under the shadow
      Of a Word, in terror or indifference, or in slow advancement,

Each body moving along the horizon of days,
      Each in its own motion, each compelled by the temporal axis,

This moving in time—Cells fueled by the heat
      Of that which is constant, but perfectly beyond all attainment—

In the presence of the Word which is nameless,
      Word which is speechless, enigma, yet gathers all unknowing

In its midst—Center of utterance, but unreachable
      With Voice—compass and goal—Shore towards which all

Telling rows, Word which is Vowelless—brutal,
      Singular portal of being—but barbed flesh of the tongue—

At time's intersection, in a state of unknowing,
      When that which is unlanguageable nears to enter the body,

Something swift—frightful—comes once under
>   The breastbone, caught in the eye's beam—something from

Without, which becomes briefly Within: Essence
>   Of attention, which drives the spine and arrests all breathing—

That something from Without: which then abandons
>   The Within—fleeting presence, brutally followed by absence;

Perfect fullness and untenable terror, which become
>   The unique nature of Desire—and the paradox for possession:

Desire for containment, but frailty of vessel—Thirst
>   For repetition—but pathless, empty, striving of will—

For the body can neither join—nor ever remain still,
>   In that great constant—captive of time and always becoming:

Therefore, unwittingly, the tongue must seek to build
>   In its wanting, the timbered structure of a word's small shape:

Thatch of marks—Wooden sanctuary for desire—
>   Thin structure of sounds to reach into the thunderous silence—

Meager house of a Word where to shelter its hunger.

INTERMEZZO

Dialogue ON THE DREAM OF THE CELESTIAL LADDER

Dialogue

ON THE DREAM OF THE CELESTIAL LADDER

I was alone. And when a figure came to me, I knew not to answer with my voice. But I understood as well how little knowledge my flesh contained. How I was suddenly empty. And my breath, slight, shallow, was the small mirror of my soul and my shame the preparation for the first rung.

And were you led out?

No. An impulse which was not thought brought me to the base of an immense ladder, and again I was pierced by the poverty of my understanding, the uselessness of my language, the penury of my love of God and all the virtues. But still I was embraced by love and so I climbed.

And what did you see from there?

I saw tiny human forms preparing their revenge, defiling the house of their brothers with their bloodshed, hiding their loathsome hearts under the cover of night. But as I climbed, I saw the earth in its expanse and variety, the great white ice caps, the vivid green and black waters—the deserts' aged thirst.

And when you looked up?

I saw that while the things of the earth were miraculous, they were nothing compared to the multiplicity of the heavenly spheres, that were the first product of energy and as I climbed the stars and planets rang out their music, and the galaxies in their ancient stone and wonder shone and revolved.

And was there air?

There was no air. Rather, there was an infinite vastness filled with the totality of history—the sum of all events which one sensed, held there in the glittering ether—alongside the brilliance of the stars and their seeming weightlessness. And one was not observed—one was part of the movement.

Did one hear?

No, or rather, one didn't hear with one's ears, but with one's being. To hear by being alongside, to hear the weight of things and to be a thing among them.

And was there time?

No, there was no time, although actions were taken in order, and as the Philosopher says, an action necessitates time. But while there were actions, there was no end to them, for the going up was an eternity. And there, emptied of time, I left behind my impatience, the sword with which I daily carved my own flesh. I left behind my vanity—which flowers among life in time—vanquished by the recognition of my own unworthiness. I left behind my jealousy as I understood from that height that misfortune is showered equally upon all.

And did you fear?

I confess, I shed not my fear. For to have lived once on earth—with its ageless and intimate terrors—is to have it still.

PART THREE

THE CELESTIAL LADDER

XVII.

Meditation

ON THE HOURS IN THE NIGHT GARDEN

I.

You have been born for this. The path laid out,
                    Your final arrival anticipated like the dry scent

Of wild lavender in Lenten light along the hill;
                    But the glorious air, all unexpected newness—

II.

You have been born for this—but unprepared,
                    The traffic of your cells carries but one desire—

To resist—this and all that is inevitable; to resist
                    That which so quickly undoes what, at the outset,

Was only so fragilely and temporally constructed;
                    But night's rugged glow against the ancient hill—

III.

The body is only at home on this earth, finally tied
                    As it is to all matter: the currents of the arteries

Wild as water coursing the river's embankment,
                Pulse constant as the globe in its spheric weight,

The planisphere of the body moving among all
                Forms—wishing to be held fast in love's gravity;

IV.

The cell's honeycomb fragile as that of wasps',
                Which hangs down midday under a branch of

Fresh laurel; *Yes*, only at home on this earth—
                And as such makes as best it can its place in it;

And love, as it does, the things of the flesh.

V.

Love: the heart's arch resistance against the
                Arbitrary—bulwark against the siege of time,

Love seeking to build, braid, knit together
                Two breaths, preciously hewn twin desires,

To hoard in Love's heat a last few minutes
                Saved from the deep, timeless hour of *after*—

VI.

For deception is harbored in each advancing
                Step—each day the scales filling with loss—

Removal, the earth's brutal renewal: the wind
                Carrying—then emptying—its store of seeds;

The heart—losing its grip, facing the approach
                To the garden, the path towards the lavender—

And the betrayal imprinted in conception's act.

XVIII.

Reading

ON THE NIGHT OF THE SECOND DAY

Warmth, for some weeks, had prepared the branches, so deep
    In their rough matrix life sparked—expanded.

    Their lengths now scored by that fragile wingèd
        Green that fills warm nights with its low flying—

In the dark of the Garden—with those new limbs bending,
    In that uneasy dark, the air hot and stiff,

    Scented by fresh rose brush and thyme, under
        A brittle spray of new stars, like His fair crown—

Nothing moved. That second night, held rock-silent before
    The Glory, where trees had risen in their

    Leafèd, curved flight—instead like waxen
        Bulbs, their blossoms were fixed in the air,

Stunned and stilled, as if firmly stayed by the knell of grief—
    Lichen, red, molded and fused—like fired

    Glass on the salty branch—Figs, ripened, held
        In the air, cast as if in rigid, aged bronze—

While the road's whiteness lay like lime: would not lift in
    The black sky—and the dry scrubs—petrified,

    Froze their veins down into the ground's silence.
        Bees' honey, resolutely, thickened to clay.

And of all of the creatures that work the earth—the ant's
    Iron hourglass was even miraculously stilled—

    Embedded as it was in that strange non-time
        Like an ancestor in amber. Above, night

Bore down on earth—mercilessly—a thick glass dome.
    While deep in the Desert, from the pierced timber

    Of the *Boswellia sacra* there fell a single resin tear.
        For it is said: the first great night of grief—

    Turns even the World's Flesh to stone.

(e)

"By analogy with self who sees the same essence everywhere . . ."

XIX.

Fragment

ON THE DISSOLUTION OF THE BODY

Each night, desire carefully tended its lamp. In
the darkness, your bodies lay together, arms and legs
entwined around love's golden center. For, having
passed through youth's growth beside the water's
damask, and having ventured beyond the shore of the
first loving voices—having cast your shadow finally,
resolutely, on the world's path—indeed this was
pleasure. To find yourself reflected, singular, in the
limitless eye of the other.

For flesh imprints its spell on the mind. In your
shared nakedness there, you observed hands, limbs and
feet—and though similar, each proclaimed its own
specificity: the brown blemish that graced the inner
thigh, the perfect, filigree script that lined the side of the
mouth, and changed in all lights—the iris's corona, with
its moats and striations, bursting in sunlight. Indeed, the
body was unique, and cherished for its oneness. And
during night's miraculous hour, each part was praised
with abandon.

Each night, desire carefully tended its lamp, and
days became years under its amber reflection. But now,
strangely, the voice of the other rang in familiar
harmony: the hand—once so particular—seemed to
mirror yours—if not in its flesh, then in its practiced

gesture. For that which the body loves, it wishes to make its own—and so between you, in the air, there rose bridges of sympathy, tying simple cell to cell and simple breath to breath.

So when grief called you, and before you lay the beloved frame, still all beauty, even in its terrible dissolution—when grief called you and you lay down in its sombre waters, or rose on its torrential current, you came to ask—with the bewilderment only of one born of the flesh—*but is this not too my hand, wrung by sweat, tried by fire? Are these not too my eyes, dark novas of still-intense desire?*

XX.

Meditation

ON FEELING THAT THE DEAD ARE NEAR

I.

And when it seems that something rises beside you,
        The air tensed and still with what you cannot name—

And the familiar room itself seems afraid, bowed
        Beneath this thickening of moment—the silence rigid

And staid—you hesitate, at this apparition of all
        That is immanent, all that is essence, yet uncontained:

For rarely can one bear witness to that which is
        The release of all that indwells, free, its shell blasted—

So surrounded—stillness to stillness—you now
        Face that which is formless—though still somehow

Tied to the world, as if longing were the filament
        Which held it here—joined to the sphere of the present:

In this moment when edge to edge near, the regions
        Of being, non-being, the realm of the dead, anxiety

Flares: even if once you had wished for this coming—
        Or thought you had—

II.

For day has watched you bend prostrate in rooms
        Where longing in countless details resolutely dwells,

And in midnight hours seen you uneasily pray,
        For the return of that one now only darkness-held:

But this presence is not the same nature as grief,
        Which is the will of the living—desiring the dead—

The dead too, have their tasks—their pilgrimage—
        And this is the Dead—willful—making their passage.

Your voice, hesitant, rises to speak: but unframed
        By qualities which would clarify presence, you ask

If it is love or mere hesitation which brings it back
        Here to the realm of the living: compelled by instinct

You manage a word, but language, dull instrument
        Is too blunt for the dead—and cuts roughly instead

The skin of the moment—and you fall, like a failed
        Hero, back to the stark wilderness of the material—

Where, your hand on the chair, you engage the bright
              Stare of the mote-filled light—in the breath-close,

      And stone-still rooms of the living.

XXI.

Commentary

ON THE 13 RUNGS OF SORROW

Daybreak

You wake to day's knowledge as Noah to the flood.

The Trial

There is no trial; but suddenly unworthy, you beg for forgiveness. None is forthcoming.

The Plea of Innocence

You seek out your own shadow; in desperation run after what you once were—after a grace of unknowing.

The Verdict

You are more fortunate than some, less than others. Destiny balances her scales. You submit to your lot.

The Sentence

The body is burned from within as if by a white flame.

The Exile

The mildness of day casts you out, and head down you walk the streets, stripped of the ability to call a name, even your own.

Night

Courage is lost in the wild dark hours when chaos swirls, and face to face with the abyss, you near the white fire of time.

Respite

You wipe your brow on the edge of daybreak.

Familiarity

You become tacit under the blows, you lament only your consciousness. A day tempered by sunlight is one held in grace's gravity.

Meditation

Now you know: wisdom is not equal to knowledge. Wisdom is knowledge to which one has been forced to submit.

The Walk in the Garden

Penetrating beyond explanations, you walk purified. Though from now until the horizon you walk cautious of being.

Silence

Still, at moments: radiance. You learn that the body in grief is privileged, and called to enter, in its rags, the immaculate garden of compassion.

The Return

If there is no sanctuary, perhaps there can be reconciliation. But the path forward is shuttered by leaves, the way once and again lengthening.

(f)
"*So it was with Job, when the veil of flesh had been rent by affliction, the world's dark beauty was revealed.*"

XXII.

Fragment

ON THE IMPROBABILITY OF WONDER
(The Melancholia)

The light was alabaster: at her feet lay all of the world's treasures—the yellow music of mathematics, and the alpha axis of the compass; the curved perfection of the globe and music's invisible colonnades; color's liquid harmonics, and the blade and the bell—all wonders laid before her, but lifeless under her inward languid gaze—

All bitter herbs—bad luck, calamity of circumstance.

Moreover for her pleasure: the magnetic needle of distance and the crystal's frozen palace; physics' blizzard of forces and logic's inlaid ivory—the affection of dogs, the astrolabe and the axe, lovers' trials and the barbed arrow of attainment—

All chains, weight, cast-up refuse—

Not even the dry ruminations of anatomy or the treacherous apex of the tetrahedron—not the sublime genius of marble, carefully shaped to buttocks and thighs: Diana's sure stone stride through air; or in the distance, the tender modulations of a mourning dove's cry—

All dross, debris, washed-up flotsam.

What use knowledge in the face of time? Her cell filled at dayfall with alabaster rays. But there at her feet, in the light ribbons the afternoon unfurled—her tears scattered, glowing, unexpectedly turned to pearls:

Sorrow's grist under contemplation: *melancholia's gem.*

XXIII.

Reading

ON THE ENDURANCE OF THE FLESH OF THE WORLD

Miraculously, weather continued its patterns—daylight
Entered each window on its vast singular

Mission; clouds rose majestic on the distant
Horizon, carrying with them libations for

The far-flung provinces. Not all storms stayed, but some
Storms lingered. Which is to say day had

Not been deformed by grief's arduous trials.
Warmth in April was again undercut by

A cool blade of wind. Autumn's return stayed rugged,
The russet, parched leaves curling; at nightfall

Soot still hung in air, and the young birches
Amid oak, shone forth like rooted lightning.

And all knowledge was still temporary, and demanded
Renewal. But the body, bearing as it did joy's

Eclipse, remained skeptical listening to the news,
Insistently denying that seas still rushed

Impatient to the harbors of the world, and that the equator
    Remained reconciled to its miraculous girth.

    Yes, despite sorrow's gravity, twilight still
        Lay liquid—slate-grey—in deep shadow,

And morning's return was luminous, in its own fashion.
    As reported to the ear, drizzle's voice endured

    Discreetly, rain's temper, incessant. Unseen,
        Water rose briefly in towers against a siege

Of wind; and sand persisted—pressed its hand into all
    The crevices of the hours: for turning as it did

    In its own tight ether, the soul knew not that,
        Even in seclusion, the elements beat true

    Against the hard frame of the mind.

NOTES

Notes

The World

(a) "Here in the body this subtle, impalpable, invisible one . . ." from *Maitri Upanishad*, in *Hindu Scriptures* (London: 1966), 277.

(b) ". . . Every process is partially or totally interfered with by chance . . ." from C. G. Jung, Introduction, *The I Ching* (New Jersey: Princeton University Press, 1977), xxii.

"On a Short History of Chance"

Among the ancient philosophers there was debate about the impact of chance on physical phenomenon. Aristotle criticized Empedocles for the extent of his use of chance in discussing regular biological phenomena. However, modern interpretations have seen Empedocles as "the first thinker to see that biology needs both randomness and principles of organization in its explanatory equipment." *The Presocratic Philosophers* (Cambridge: Cambridge University Press, 1993), 307.

The Temple

"On a Panel of Adam Naming the Animals"

Dolor mortalis: human pain.

(c) "An angel of God taught him Hebrew, the language of revelation . . ." from *The Jewish Encyclopedia* (New York: Funk, 1901), 85.

"On the Struggle with the Angel"

In certain medieval literature one finds an interpretation of Jacob's struggle with the Angel not as an encounter with an external divine being, but rather the internal struggle of the self with consciousness.

(d) *"He then takes virgin soil from a mountain which has not been dug by men . . ."* from Louis Jacobs, *The Jewish Religion* (Oxford: Oxford University Press, 1995), 197.

"On the Creation of the Golem"

In addition to the Jewish mystical sources, I am indebted in this poem to Hannah Arendt's writing in *The Human Condition:* "Man . . . seems to be possessed by a rebellion against human existence as it has been given, a free gift from nowhere . . . which he wishes to exchange . . . for something he has made himself. There is no reason to doubt our abilities to accomplish such an exchange, just as there is no reason to doubt our present ability to destroy all organic life on earth." Hannah Arendt, *The Human Condition* (Chicago: University of Chicago Press, 1958), 2–3.

"Dialogue on the Dream of the Celestial Ladder"

Over the centuries there have been many written and graphic depictions of the ascent of the Celestial Ladder. Among these are Jacob's famous dream, the very rich western medieval tradition, as well as texts such as *Liber Scale Machometi, The Book of Mohammed's Ladder.* For the writing of this book, I am indebted to the appearance of the ladder in the form of an inverted cross with numerous transecting beams, an ancient symbol of the soul's pilgrimage from earthly existence towards paradise.

THE CELESTIAL LADDER

"On the Hours in the Night Garden"

In the Mediterranean basin, *Tournefort,* or French lavender (*Lavandula stoechas*), blooms from March to May.

"On the Night of the Second Day"

This poem is a *fantasia* on Holy Saturday, the day situated between Good Friday and Easter Sunday. The "*Boswellia sacra*" is the Latin name for the tree, found in the Near East, which produces the precious resin frankincense.

(e) *"By analogy with self who sees the same essence everywhere . . ."* The *Bhagavad-Gita*, in *Hindu Scriptures* (London: 1966), 348.

"On the Dissolution of the Body"

This poem is influenced by readings of the sacred Hindu texts, in particular the Upanishads.

It is dedicated to Khoa Pham, in memory of Cornelis Timmerman.

(f) "So it was that to Job, when once the veil of flesh had been rent . . ." from Simone Weil, "The Love of God and Affliction" in *The Simone Weil Reader* (New York: David McKay Company, 1977), 456. Reprinted permission of Moyer Bell, Ltd.

"On the Improbability of Wonder"

In certain representations of the *melancholia*, characteristics of this meditating female figure are mixed with symbols relating to the repentant Mary Magdalen. Among the Magdalen's symbols is an alabaster jar filled with oil.

Drawing on the tradition of the *Vita Contemplativa*, the form of *The White Fire of Time* reflects some of the preoccupations of its deeper sources. The first and third sections follow a MRFMCFR pattern, while the central section is MRFCMCFRM. In general, poems of similar type have the same or similar length, and often are variations on a specific prosodic or philosophical concern.

The Celestial Ladder is dedicated to the memory of
Dorothy Leeds Werner Hinsey,
murdered May 21, 1990.

I would like to express my gratitude to those individuals who gave
valuable criticism and support during the years when this book was
being written: in the United States, my family; L.S., S.L. and N.M.;
in Paris, T.P., G.N., A.C. *et les autres, amis exiles, et exilés.*

With deep gratitude to C. who lifted me up.

Et infiniement et toujours, M.C.

Index